How to W. t Sell

A Simple Formula

By

Christina Palmer

About the author

Christina is a part-time author and full time mother and wife. In March 2012 she published her first erotic short story, "Taking Jenny" on Kindle Direct Publishing and has since sold over 50,000 books on Amazon and other digital publishing platforms.

This is Christina's first foray into non-fiction and is based on the experience she has gained and the formula she used to become one of the most widely read self-published erotic short story writers of the last year.

Table of contents

Foreword (by Bianca James)

Introduction - My journey

Foreword

The desire to write has burned within me from the time I was a small child and wrote my first story on my Mom's computer. I knew it was what I wanted to do, but as I got older, life seemed to get in the way and my dreams were pushed aside.

Throughout a variety of careers, I worked in my spare time as a freelance magazine writer to satisfy my creative urges, but deep down I knew I wanted to do more than write articles about real estate or computer software. I'd never written fiction before and was too afraid of failing to attempt it.

Stumbling across Christina Palmer's "How to Write Erotic Short Stories that Sell", while searching Amazon for 'how to' books on writing, was a light bulb moment for me. I bought the book, absorbed Christina's easy step by step formula and read the sample short stories which put the formula into practice. I was hooked and had the blueprint; I knew I was ready to give it a try.

My first attempt at erotic fiction was a 10,000 word short story Stranger Addiction (Awakening Sophy: Part One), which I published in May 2013 in the hope that I would sell a few hundred copies within a few months to cover my editing and cover design costs. That milestone was reached in two weeks and sales grew exponentially from there, taking me to 44 on the Top 100 Best Sellers in Erotica chart with a sales ranking of around 1,000 soon after.

Encouraged by this success and having sold over 3,500 copies of my first story in only 2 months, I published a second story Public Obsession (Awakening Sophy: Part Two), which followed the same sales and ranking path as Part One, using exactly the same formula.

I'm now working on Parts Three and Four with plans for many other short stories and even a full length novel in the pipeline.

I cannot recommend the formula shared by Christina highly enough, it really works, I've proven that and you can too!

Good luck and get writing!

Bianca James

Introduction (My Journey)

In March 2012 my husband asked me out of the blue, "when are you going to rewrite your manuscript and take it to a publisher?" To be honest I groaned. I had explored this opportunity many times, only to find myself, like many others, knocking my head against a brick wall. The gates of traditional publishing were well guarded and notoriously hard to break through. I had given up completely over two years before, my novel left unfinished sitting somewhere in a dark corner of my hard drive. I was much too busy with children and a career to pursue something that seemed impossible.

On a whim though, I decided to research self-publishing on the internet. Of course I had looked into this option before but that was before the advent of the modern day form. Back when I had first explored it, self-publishing was basically paying to have your book printed and bound in paperback form and pay thousands, perhaps tens of thousands for a few hundred copies that you would then have to sell yourself, hoping to recoup your costs and dreaming of being picked up by a traditional publisher.

That day in 2012, I stumbled across the "self-publishing revolution". Amazon, Smashwords and Barnes and Noble had all taken things to another level. It was now possible to self-publish with a minimum of fuss and outlay AND have immediate access to an immense and growing market, E-books. In 2011 E-book sales overtook print book sales for the first time and have grown exponentially since. Words like

Kindle, Nook and e-reader have now become a part of our everyday vernacular.

Of course, the more I discovered about self-publishing e-books the more I liked and the deeper I delved. In the course of my research I read about authors who had broken through to make bestseller lists and of course the name on everyone's lips at that time, was E.L. James. So in conjunction with my (long overdue) discovery that self-publishing was easier than ever, erotica had gone mainstream and the person leading the way was a self-published super success story.

Now, my unfinished novel is most definitely not erotica but I have always loved the genre. I had type written many erotic short stories for my husband and he had enjoyed them immensely. I honestly think that reading erotica has a place as a healthy sexual aid, both for individuals and well balanced couples. As I sat reading about "Shades of Grey", its three volumes sat 1, 2 and 3 on the bestseller lists and I thought to myself, I CAN DO THIS! Not only could I do it, I had a small catalogue of short erotica that I had sitting in the drawer and could polish up immediately.

The first story I started with was one I had written about a wife who receives a knock on the door one night while her husband is away on business and finds her sister's husband on the doorstep. Puzzled she invites him in and he proceeds to blackmail her into sex. I rewrote this with a few changes (sister's husband became her boyfriend) and it became the first of my published stories and also the first of my top 100 bestsellers on Amazon, Taking Jenny. It was so well received that I decided to make it into a novel (Duty Bound - The Enslavement of Jenny) as I had lots of ideas of how the story of Jenny could proceed. Taking inspiration from other authors, I decided to serialise it and released it over the course of six months in five more instalments, Breaking Jenny, Training Jenny, Sharing Jenny, Punishing Jenny and Jenny Unbound.

Doing this enabled me to break down the story into bite sized chunks while preserving the short story feel of each instalment. Turns out, I could do it and each of the Jenny stories sold quickly and well beyond my expectations. Between the release of Taking Jenny on March 14 2012 and today I have sold over 30,000 copies of the entire Duty Bound – Enslavement of Jenny series and the box set on Amazon alone, and have surpassed 50,000 sales of all of my books on all platforms since beginning just last year.

The success of the Jenny series and another, "The Bad Cop Trilogy", convinced me that what I did best and what sold well, was erotic short stories and that is where I have concentrated my efforts. I have learnt new things every time I have published and received feedback from readers and friends and family, but my greatest lesson of all, is that you can't please everybody.

Some people love the hard-core nature of some of my stories, others don't and in fact I have been accused of encouraging women to be treated as nothing more than sex objects, destroying the sanctity of marriage and various other unfair assertions. I write sex fantasy, none of the things in my stories have ever happened to me, I write too titillate and for escapism and nothing more.

My main rules are now to write what I want to write, what I write well and perhaps what I think my husband will like. If you stick to those rules, you are starting from a solid platform. In the following pages I will hopefully impart some of my experiences, structure and strategy and enable you to dabble your toes in the world of short erotic stories and perhaps make some money doing it.

Chapter 1

Why would you write short erotica?

Well I have a theory on this. To me erotic fiction is really all about short stories. Let's face it, a novel is hard work, and you can't just write 100,000 words of non-stop sex, you have to have a story that you want to tell and then you have to weave the erotica into and through the storyline. That is all well and good, but I guess there are two types of erotica consumers, Type A- those who want *erotica* with a story and Type B- the ones who primarily want a *story* with erotica.

In my experience it is Type A that will buy and consume short erotic stories. They are buying it for the *sex*- the titillation and excitement of a dirty story. They know they are going to get sex and *hopefully* sex with a good story to it. I'm a type A. If I go browsing for erotica, I am looking for a subject that will turn me on and is well written, with a believable storyline and characters. I believe a Type B is looking for a good long story with more detailed characters and an involved storyline along with some sexy scenes to keep the narrative rolling.

Why is short erotica so effective in this ever popular genre? Well think about it, it fits perfectly. When I break down my formula for writing a short erotic story, it is almost like the act of sex itself. Introduction and build-up (foreplay), the main act, (the act of sex itself) and then the conclusion (postcoital) lay back on the pillows and decide it's a one off or talk about the next time. Let's face it, every story has to have a beginning, a middle and an end, and in short erotica, this is literally *all there is*.

Let's break down **Sharing Emma – The Collared Slut** (Spoiler alert) in its basic form. (the full story is available in the final chapter if you would like to read it before continuing).

Introduction (foreplay):

We find Jeremy starting his shift as waiter in an exclusive London restaurant. He discovers that a patron has booked out "the nook", an exclusive three table room and that he, Jeremy, will be waiting on him. The patron is a distinguished older man and on his arm is the most gorgeous girl that Jeremy has ever laid eyes upon. An odd couple to be sure. The reader is teased when the old gentleman has his "date" do certain things that are just not done in public; several of these things involve Jeremy as the old man begins to *share* Emma.

Main act (Sex):

Jeremy is enamoured with the girl and her submissiveness and is easily talked into continuing the evening when the old man pays to have the entire restaurant at his disposal after closing. Not only does Jeremy get to share Emma, but an attractive couple, lured by the promise of debauchery also join in. What follows is a fairly straight forward group sex scene, spiced up by the absolute submissiveness of the titular character.

Conclusion (Postcoital):

It's done, sex has been had, the participants and the reader are satisfied. Here we explore briefly the feelings of the main characters and wrap up the story (they lived happily ever after) or leave the story open for a sequel or another instalment. In the conclusion to Sharing Emma, Jeremy is disappointed she fails to meet his eyes as she is leaving, but the story has the possibility of more to come, when he is handed a business card by her "owner".

The point I'm trying to make, is that well written short erotica can easily be mapped if you have great story ideas, good character development and can write well. We will look more at the structure of a short erotic story (my way) in chapter 3.

Chapter 2

Who should write it?

The answer to this is *you*, if you meet a few criteria. Firstly you're reading this book, that should be enough to get you started by at least putting your feet upon the path, it means you are interested in writing and publishing erotica. You will need more than just interest though, and in order I would list the following:

- A love of reading

If you don't read for pleasure, you will have little chance of writing anything that anybody else will read. I don't know of ANY writer of note that did not start upon their chosen path by first falling in love with books and reading.

- A love of writing

Ideally you would have already written or at least started lots of written work. I could be anything, sci-fi, romance, self-help etc. Apart from the erotic short stories I had written for my husband, I had started at least six novels that never made the cut, but the fact was, each of them was a step along the learning curve. If you have never even thought of writing I would stop right now if I were you, but of course nothing is impossible.

- A love of sex

Let's face it, if you don't have a love and appreciation of good sex and a variety of kinks, the chances are you will never be able to write about it in a convincing and engaging manner.

-    A muse

Is there a significant other in your life that you write for or would write for in order to arouse and titillate? I recommend for your first few stories you have this person in mind as your reader. The one you are trying to excite. Think about what they like and use that as the springboard for your first story. When you finish your first draft, give it to them and see if it achieves what you are aiming for.

Of course you may not tick all of these boxes and still, in fact, be able to write good erotica, writing is after all a skill that can be learned, but I have found that the passion behind the words is generally the difference between good erotica and excellent erotica.

A word of warning:

Don't let money be your only motivation in beginning to write erotica. You have to do it because you want to do it and enjoy doing it, otherwise this will filter through to your work and on to your readers. Passion cannot be faked.

Chapter 3

How to do it, including a study of Taking Jenny

Note: The full current edition of Taking Jenny is located at the back of this book, you may wish to read it before you continue, but it is not absolutely necessary.

Taking Jenny was the first story I published and was taken from one I had written for my husband years earlier. I had written it for the express purpose of turning him on; it contained blackmail, semi-taboo forced sex between a woman and her sister's husband and graphic sex scenes. It worked, he loved it and we read that story together several times (you know what I mean).

So I dusted it off and polished it up. I changed the ending and some of the content so that it could continue on as a saga of domination and submission and self-published it through Amazon's KDP (Kindle Direct Publishing) program. I was quite ecstatic when I sold three copies on the first day it was available. I felt I had been validated and began work on the sequel immediately and the rest, as they say, is history.

We will now look at the structure of Taking Jenny and how I have made its "formula" the blueprint for all of my short stories.

Introduction (foreplay):

We find Jenny waving goodbye to her husband as he leaves on his business trip. We learn that she is worried about the state of her marriage and the financial problems created by the GFC. We also discern through the reactions of the teenage boy next door that she is attractive and desirable. Later, as she relaxes, she is a little tipsy after a few glasses of wine and is aroused to the point that she decides to masturbate. We follow this along, teasing the reader *and* the protagonist (Jenny) before interrupting her solo fun with the doorbell.

Standing at the door is Mike, her sister's boyfriend. He looks uneasy and is holding a laptop computer. Jenny, surprised at the late night visit invites him in and offers him a cup of coffee. Cutting to the chase he opens his computer and directs Jenny to watch a video that he plays. It is Jenny, performing a sex act with a strange man. Horrified, Jenny rails at Mike, asking where he got the video. That is beside the point for Mike, the fact is that he has it and will forward it to Brad and everyone in his office for all to see if she doesn't comply with his wishes. The real purpose of his visit is now revealed.

We have achieved a few things to this point. We've introduced Jenny, established that she is an attractive and sexual being and also that she is having marriage difficulties. Importantly, we've also established a sexual expectation (*sexpectation*) for the reader of what they can look forward to in the main act. (We have also tapped a few things that maybe familiar to readers, interrupted masturbation, the fear of a late night caller and blackmail being the main ones.)

Main act (Sex):

After initially resisting and begging, Jenny relents and is violated by Mike. He pulls no sexual punches as he takes advantage of her vulnerability. Surprisingly, after her initial shock, Jenny responds physically to the way he is treating her and finds herself enjoying the fierce sex. As her sexual arousal and excitement peaks, she becomes a willing participant in the sex and encourages Mike to treat her like a whore as he violates her first in the kitchen and then in her marital bed.

Conclusion (Postcoital):

As they recover from the exhausting sex, Mike reiterates his threats and makes it clear that he is not finished with Jenny. Jenny, for her part, is revolted at her reaction to the way he has treated her but is also aroused by the thought of what is to come. The ending leads and points to a follow up, hopefully hooking your reader into purchasing the next instalment.

That is the **basic** structure of Taking Jenny, translating this to your story will be easy enough if you follow the following recipe:

Introduction:

Introduce your protagonist and provide a basic overview of them including a description, their current life situation (marital status/ issues/ work) and lead into the main act, describing the immediate situation, i.e. what is happening (Jenny masturbating, then being interrupted by a mysterious knock at the door) and the promise of what is yet to come, (Mike acting strange and revealing his blackmail). The introduction will detail the motives of your protagonist and antagonist. It will define why we are heading towards sex and whether it is reluctant or willing and whether your character is aggressive or passive. The idea of the introduction is to set the scene and create a certain amount of tension.

Main act:

Sex and its lead up. This is the meat of your story, the point your introduction drove the narrative towards. It needs to be about 80% of your word count, this is why your reader is reading and it has to satisfy. Depending on the style/ situation, it is best to keep things simple here. For a straight out boy meets girl has sex story, you would start slowly and build towards a climax. In the case of Taking Jenny, it had to be less subtle due to the situation but you will see as you read it that it takes the slow approach – he makes her strip, touches and teases her (pseudo foreplay) before the main act of sex (penetration) occurs. You don't need to limit yourself to one scene at all, as you can see; Mike dragging Jenny to the bedroom for a second round works well but is in keeping with the story.

Conclusion:

This should be approximately 5% of your word count. It is designed to close the story by wrapping it up in a tidy way. Here is where your characters will debrief and if applicable make plans/ infer that there will be another story to come. You will illustrate their feelings after the act and how they feel about the whole situation (*After he had gone, Jenny, still dazed, walked back into her bedroom and sat on the bed.*

There was a ball of dread in her stomach at the predicament she was in, but behind that there was also excitement. Anticipation of what Mike had in store for her.).

Don't drag this part of the story out; it should say just enough to leave a nice tidy ending or a hook to the next instalment for the reader.

Notes

Chapter 4

Nuts and bolts/ Ideas and words

Okay, so we have looked at the basic architecture of our short story, but the things holding it together are your words and ideas. You of course will have your own ideas, whether they come from experiences you've already had or want to have, things you've heard about or ideas from other sources like pornography. You should also be influenced by who your target audience is. The ideas or scenarios you come up with should be tailored to the audience you are trying to reach.

On the whole, women aren't looking for lesbian, hard-core gangbangs or fantasy rape scenarios; however men will definitely search them out. On the other hand, men aren't likely to enjoy overtly soft-core scenarios like a wife's illicit love affair. There are exceptions to both rules though. My books are generally geared towards both males and females and yet some of the best reviews for my harder style stories (The Bad Cop for example) have come from women.

The basic rule as to how and what audience you will gear your story towards is "use your own judgement." It will also pay to research the top 100 erotica lists, see what's selling and who is writing the reviews for an added feel.

Once you have your target audience and your scenario, it's time to look at your words. If you're writing for women, subtle is the key word. My story "While the Cat's Away…" is one that I geared specifically towards a female audience and you will see that the language and scenario is quite different to say Taking Jenny or Sharing Emma.

Women on the whole don't want pussies, cocks, fucks and cunts. They want sex, shafts, hard members and penetration. It's about being descriptive and sexy without bludgeoning the reader.

Men on the other hand don't mind being hit over the head with a few juicy adjectives and verbs. Look at the two ways this paragraph is written and see if you can pick which one is tailored to men and which to women.

"She gasped as his member began to grow in her hand. He looked at her intently, a half smile playing at his lips as she began to slowly move her hand up and down his shaft. Excited at the effect she was having on the professor and unable to contain herself any longer, she closed her lips over the head of his beautiful manhood and tilted her head back as he slid the full length of it into her compliant and wet mouth."

"He saw a look of surprise on her face as his cock began to grow in her soft hand. He looked at her intently, a half smile on his lips as she began to rub the engorged length of it. Horny at the effect she was having on the professor and unable to contain her inner slut any longer, she closed her mouth over the head of his thick cock and began to suck it vigorously, gagging slightly as it banged against the back of her throat."

You can see how with just a few words, the entire complexion/ tone of the paragraph can be changed completely. The second is more graphic and visual, while the first much more subtle and soft.

As to sentence structure, tense, and point of view, I will leave that to you, this is not a how to write book and I'm assuming if you've come this far you know how to write. I would say that in short erotic stories, brief punchy descriptions and sentences can be very effective for maintaining a fast pace and compelling narrative.

The next chapter contains a simple thesaurus that may help you expand your erotic vocabulary.

<u>Notes</u>

.

Chapter 5 – Erotic Thesaurus

Arouse - agitate, awaken, attract, charm, coax, electrify, enliven, entice, excite, fire up, foment, fuel, goad, heat up, incite, inflame, instigate, kindle, lure, produce, provoke, rouse, spark, stimulate, stir, tantalize, tease, tempt, thrill, torment, waken, warm

Assault - abuse, assail, attack, bombard, inundate, invade, onslaught, overwhelm, violate

Beautiful - alluring, angelic, appealing, attractive, beguiling, bewitching, charming, captivating, dazzling, delicate, delightful, divine, elegant, enchanting, engaging, enthralling, enticing, exquisite, eye-catching, fascinating, fetching, fine, fine-looking, good-looking, gorgeous, graceful, handsome, inviting, lovely, magnificent, marvellous, mesmerizing, pleasing, pretty, radiant, rakish, ravishing, refined, resplendent, splendid, striking, stunning, sublime, tantalizing, tempting

Brutal - atrocious, barbarous, bestial, brutish, callous, cold-blooded, cruel, fierce, feral, ferocious, heartless, hard, harsh, inhuman, merciless, murderous, nasty, pitiless, rancorous, remorseless, rough, rude, ruthless, sadistic, savage, severe, terrible, uncompromising, unfeeling, unforgiving, unmerciful, unpitying, vicious, violent, wild

Carnal - animalistic, bodily, coarse, crude, dirty, filthy, impure, lascivious, lecherous, lewd, libidinous, licentious, lustful, physical, prurient, raunchy, rough, salacious, sensuous, unclean, voluptuous, vulgar, wanton

Dangerous - acute, alarming, critical, damaging, deadly, death-defying, deathly, destructive, detrimental, explosive, fatal, formidable, grave, harmful, hazardous, injurious impending, lethal, life-threatening, malignant, menacing, mortal, nasty, noxious, perilous, poisonous, precarious, pressing, risky, serious, severe, terrible, terrifying, threatening, toxic, treacherous, unsafe, unstable, urgent, venomous, vulnerable, wicked

Delicious - appetizing, delectable, enticing, exquisite, flavoursome, full of flavour, juicy, lip-smacking, luscious, lush, mouth-watering, piquant, relish, rich, ripe, salty, savorier, scrummy, scrumptious, spicy, succulent, sweet, tangy, tart, tasty, tempting, yummy, zesty

Disturbing -alarming, appalling, atrocious, baleful, bizarre, bleak, bloodcurdling, boding evil, chilling, cold, condemned, creepy, damned, daunting, demented, desolate, dire, doomed, dour, dismal, disturbing, dread, dreary, dusk, eerie, fear, fearsome, frightening, ghastly, ghostly, ghoulish, gloom, gloomy, grave, grim, grisly, gruesome, hair-raising, haunted, hideous, hopeless, horrendous, horrible, horrid, horrific, horrifying, horror, ill-fated, ill-omened, ill-starred, inauspicious, inhospitable, looming, lost, macabre, malice, malignant, menacing, murky, mysterious, night, panic, pessimistic, petrifying, scary, shade, shadows, shadowy, shady, shocking, soul-destroying, sour, spine-chilling, spine-tingling, strange, terrifying, uncanny, unearthly, unlucky, unnatural, unnerving, weird, wretched

Ecstasy - bliss, blissful, delectation, delighted, delirious, delirium, elated, elation, enraptured, excitement, extremely happy, euphoria, euphoric, fervent, fervour, frenzied, frenzy, happiness, heaven, high, in raptures (of delight), in seventh heaven, joy, joyous, jubilant, on cloud nine, overexcited, overjoyed, paradise, rapture, rapturous, rhapsody, thrill, thrilled, transported, wild

Erotic - amatory, amorous, aphrodisiac, carnal, earthy, erogenous, fervid, filthy, hot, impassioned, lascivious, lecherous, lewd, raw, romantic, rousing, salacious, seductive, sensual, sexual, spicy, steamy, stimulating, suggestive, tantalizing, titillating, voluptuous

Evil - abominable, amoral, atrocious, awful, bad, base, criminal, cruel, dangerous, barbarous, debased, deplorable, depraved, despicable, devious, distressing, dreadful, evil, fearful, fiendish, fierce, foul, hazardous, heartless, heinous, ill-intentioned, immoral, impious, impish, indecent, iniquitous, intense, irreverent, loathsome, Machiavellian, mad, malevolent, malicious, mean, merciless, mischievous, monstrous, nasty, naughty, nefarious, offensive, perverse, profane, ruthless, scandalous, severe, shameful, shameless, sinful, spiteful, terrible, uncaring, unholy, unkind, unscrupulous, vicious, vile, villainous, vindictive, virulent, wayward, wicked, wretched

Gasp - breath, choke, gulp, heave, huff, inhale, intake, pant, puff, rasp, sharp intake of air, short of breath, snort, struggle for breath, swallow, winded, wheeze

Heated - ablaze, aflame, all-consuming, ardent, avid, blazing, blistering, burning, crazed, excited, explosive, febrile, fervent, fervid, feverish, fierce, fiery, fired up, flaming, flushed, frantic, frenzied, furious, hot, hot-blooded, impassioned, impatient, incensed, intense, maddening, obsessed, passionate, possessed, raging, randy, scalding, scorching, searing, sizzling, smouldering, stormy, sweltering, tempestuous, torrid, turbulent, vehement, violent, volatile, worked up, zealous

Hungry - ache, appetite, avaricious, avid, carnivorous, covetous, craving, desirous, eager, famished, gluttony, grasping, greed, greedy, hungered, insatiable, keen, longing, lust, mania, mouth-watering, predatory, rapacious, ravenous, ravening, starved, starving, thirst, thirsty, unsatisfied, voracious, want, wanting, yearning

Intense - acute, agonizing, anxious, ardent, biting, bitter, burning, close, consuming, cutting, deep, eager, earnest, excessive, exquisite, extreme, fervent, fervid, fierce, forceful, forcible, great, harsh, impassioned, keen, marked, passionate, piercing, powerful, profound, severe, sharp, strong, vehement, vigorous, violent, vivid

Liquid - aqueous, awash, cream, creamy, damp, dewy, drenched, drip, dripping, drop, droplet, drowning, elixir, extract, flood, flooded, flowing, fountain, flux, jewel, juice, juicy, leaky, liquor, luscious, melted, milky, moist, moisture, nectar, overflowing, pulpy, sap, sappy, saturated, sauce, secretion, slick, slippery, soaked, soaking, sodden, soggy, solvent, sopping, stream, succulent, swamp, tear, teardrop, torrent, viscous, vitae, waterlogged, watery, weeping, wet

Limber - agile, deft, fit, flexible, lanky, lean, leggy, lithe, lissom, nimble, pliant, sinewy, sinuous, sleek, slender, slight, slim, skinny, spare, supple, svelte, thin, trim, willowy, wiry

Moving - affecting, affective, arousing, awakening, awe-inspiring, breathless, dynamic, eloquent, emotional, emotive, energizing, exciting, exhilarating, expressive, far-out, fascinating, fecund, felt in gut, grabbed by, gripping, heartbreaking, heart pounding, heartrending, heart stopping, impelling, impressive, inspirational, inspiring, meaningful, mind-bending, mind-blowing, motivating, persuasive, poignant, propelling, provoking, quickening, rallying, riveting, rousing, significant, simulative, stimulating, stirring, stunning, thrilling, touching

Need - ache, addiction, appetite, aspiration, avid, burn, compulsion, craving, demand, desire, desperate, devoir, eagerness, extremity, fascination, fever, fixation, greed, hankering, hope, hunger, impatient, impulse, inclination, infatuation, insatiable, itch, longing, lust, must, obsession, passion, pining, taste, thirst, urge, urgency, voracious, want, wish, yearning, yen

Pain - ache, afflict, affliction, agonize, agony, angry, anguish, arduous, awful, biting, bleeding, bloody, burning, bruised, caustic, chafing, cutting, distress, dire, dreadful, excruciating, extreme, fever, grief, grievous, hurt, inflamed, injured, irritated, misery, pang, piercing, prickly, punish, raw, sensitive, severe, sharp, skinned, smarting, sore, sting, suffering, tender, terrible, throb, throbbing, throe, torment, torture, tormenting, unbearable, uncomfortable, upsetting, wounded

Penis - cock, flesh, hardness, hard-on, manhood, male hardness, meat, member, pole, rod, shaft,

Perverted - aberrant, abhorrent, abnormal, base, corrupt, debased, debauched, decadent, defiling, degrading, degenerate, depraved, deviant, dirty, disgusting, dissipated, dissolute, distasteful, hedonistic, immodest, immoral, indecent, indulgent, licentious, monstrous, nasty, profligate, repellent, repugnant, repulsive, revolting, shameful, shameless, sick, sinful, smutty, sordid, tainted, twisted, unscrupulous, vicious, vile, warped, wicked

Pleasant - adventure, agreeable, amusement, bliss, buzz, charming, contentment, delicious, delight, delightful, desire, ecstasy, enjoyable, enjoyment, excitement, fun, gluttony, gratifying, happiness, harmony, heaven, joy, kick, liking, luscious, nice, paradise, pleasure, pleasurable, pleasing, relish, satisfaction, satisfying, savoury, seventh heaven, soothing, succulent, thrilling

Powerful - able-bodied, athletic, beefy, big, brawny, broad-shouldered, bulky, enormous, great, hard, hardy, hearty, heavily built, heavy, hefty, huge, husky, massive, mighty, muscular, outsized, oversized, powerfully built, prodigious, robust, solid, stalwart, stocky, strapping, strong, strongly built, sturdy, thick, thickset, tough, well-built, well-developed

Rigid - definite, firm, fixed, hard, harsh, immovable, inflexible, obstinate, resolved, resolute, rigorous, severe, solid, steady, stern, stiff, strict, strong, stubborn, taut, tense, tight, tough, unbending, unchangeable, uncompromising, unrelenting, unwavering, unyielding

Sudden - abrupt, accelerated, acute, brash, brisk, brusque, fast, flashing, fleeting, hasty, headlong, hurried, immediate, impetuous, impulsive, instant, instantaneous, out of the blue, quick, quickening, rapid, rash, reckless, rushed, rushing, sharp, spontaneous, swift, urgent, without warning

Squirm - agonize, angle, arc, bend, bow, buck, coil, contort, convulse, curl, curve, fidget, fight, flex, go into spasm, grind, heave, jerk, jiggle, jolt, lash, lash out, kick, lurch, plunge, rear, recoil, reel, ripple, resist, roll, screw up, shake, shift, slide, slither, spasm, squirm, stir, strain, stretch, struggle, suffer, surge, swell, swivel, thrash, thresh, thrust, turn violently, tussle, twist, twitch, undulate, warp, worm, wiggle, wrench, wrestle, wriggle, writhe, yank

Thrust - advance, drive, forge, forward, impetus, impulsion, lunge, momentum, onslaught, poke, power, pressure, proceed, prod, progress, propel, propulsion, punch, push, shove

Taken aback - aghast, amazed, astonished, astounded, awestruck, bewildered, confounded, dazed, dismayed, dumbfounded, flabbergasted, gob-smacked, horrified, incredulous, overwhelmed, shocked, staggered, startled, stunned, surprised

Tease - afflict, agony, angst, anguish, conflict, distress, grief, heartache, hurt, misery, misfortune, nightmare, pain, punishment, sorrow, strife, suffering, test, trial, tribulation, torment, torture, turmoil, persecute, vex, woe

Touch - bite, blow, brush, bump, buss, burrow, bury, caress, circle, collide, claw, clean, clutch, come together, contact, converge, cover, crash, creep, crush, cuddle, cup, curl, delve, dig, drag, draw, ease, edge, embrace, feel, feel up, fiddle with, finger, flick, flit, fondle, frisk, fumble, glance, glide, graze, grind, grip, grope, grub, handle, hit, hold, huddle, hug, impact, join, junction, kiss, knead, lap, lave, lay a hand on, lick, line, manipulate, manhandle, manoeuvre, mash, massage, march, meet, muzzle, neck, nestle, nibble, nip, nudge, nuzzle, outline, palm, partake, pat, paw, peck, pet, pinch, play, polish, press, probe, pull, push, rasp, ravish, reach, ream, rim, rub, run, scratch, scoop, scrabble, scrape, scrub, shave, shift, skate, skim, slide, slip, slither, smack, smooth, snake, snuggle, soothe, spank, splay, spread, squeeze, stretch, strike, stroke, suck, shunt, sweep, swipe, tag, tangle, tap, taste, tease, thumb, thump, tickle, tip, tongue, toy, touching, trace, trail, tug, tunnel, twiddle, twirl, twist, work, wrap

Vagina - beaver, bush, cunt, gash, lips, pussy, quim, slit, snatch, womanhood, opening, vulva

Wet - bathe, bleed, burst, cascade, cream, course, cover, damp, dampen, deluge, dip, douse, drench, dribble, drip, drool, drop, drown, drizzle, dunk, erupt, flood, flow, gush, immerse, issue, jet, leach, leak, moisten, ooze, overflow, permeate, plunge, pour, rain, rinse, run, salivate, saturate, secrete, seep, shower, shoot, slaver, slobber, slop, slosh, sluices, soak, souse, spew, spill, spit, splash, splatter, spout, spray, sprinkle, spurt, squirt, steep, stream, submerge, surge, swab, swamp, swill, swim, trickle, wash, water

<u>Notes</u>

Chapter 6 and Conclusion

I decided the best way to end this book was to include two full short stories. Taking Jenny and Sharing Emma. Taking Jenny was geared towards a mixed audience, whilst Sharing Emma is more for men and has a man as the central character/ protagonist.

Whether you like them or not is unimportant, the bottom line is that they both illustrate my formula in practice. As you read, see if you can pick the transitions between introduction, main act and conclusion and also note the descriptive language used in in the sex scenes.

Finally, I would like to give you a few tips. Always have someone you trust read your story after it is completed (first draft). You want to know if the story flowed and made sense and also if it was sexually stimulating. Take on board suggestions and rewrite if necessary. Then rewrite it again.

When you have completed your third draft, give it to someone to edit. That is, either pay someone or have someone with extensive reading experience and a good eye for detail read it for you. I use a publishing service called QuickQuills Editing (jane-writer.wix.com/quick-quills-editing) who I find ideal for short stories, they are reasonably priced and easy to deal with. If you insist on doing your own editing, make sure after you are happy with your finished product you have it read to you, either by someone you know, or preferably by computer software. I use free downloadable software and there are many available on the market. You will be amazed how many errors your naked eye missed when you hear your story read to you.

Good luck and happy writing, I hope you found this guide a valuable tool on your trip to self-published glory.

Complete Story Samples

TAKING JENNY

Jenny squinted into the late afternoon sun, waving to Brad as he backed the Prius down the drive. She had mixed emotions, this was his third business trip to New York in as many months and Jenny was concerned that it didn't bother her. Not even a little. If anything she felt a sense of relief.

She gave one final wave as Brad's car disappeared and turned to go back inside, but not before she spied her neighbour's pimply teenage son, Daniel, ogling her as he raked leaves on their front lawn. Jenny smiled radiantly and gave him a wave that he awkwardly returned before continuing with his chore. Jenny chuckled softly as she gracefully climbed the stairs to her front door. At thirty-four the attractive brunette could easily have passed for a woman ten years younger. The soft waves of her chocolate coloured hair fell around her shoulders, contrasting her creamy complexion perfectly. She was wearing a red and white rugby jersey and a pair of tight blue jeans that hugged her curves flatteringly.

As she turned to close the door, she saw that Daniel's eyes were again upon her and she smiled inwardly when he turned away guiltily. It was nice to have some validation of her attractiveness, something that was sorely lacking in her marriage right now. She went down the hall and into the kitchen, flicking on the coffee percolator before sitting down at the table. Her mind wandered. Why didn't she feel upset that Brad was gone again? Perhaps it was her fault? They had been married now for six years, and it seemed that while both of them had their successful careers, nothing seemed to matter, they had money to burn and lived an extravagant lifestyle with scarcely a boring moment. Then the GFC had struck and Jenny's advertising firm had gone under during the worst of the downturn.

It had been over three years now, and although she managed to keep herself busy during the days by searching for permanent work and doing the occasional freelance job, the nights had become more and more strained. Jenny was bored and unsatisfied with her life, and it didn't help that the spice had gone out of their marriage. Brad had become more and more involved with his work and was tired and snappy in the evenings. The spontaneity had completely disappeared and the nights now blended into one another, a relentless march of boring evenings, filled with television, bland conversation and petty arguments.

More worryingly, their sex life had withered and almost died. Jenny was always the instigator now, and increasingly Brad rejected her advances, a situation that would have been unthinkable even a year ago. Perhaps then, it was no surprise that she should feel relief that he was gone for a couple of nights, for a little while, she could put away the gnawing feeling that it was all coming to end and be by herself.

That night, after eating a light meal with a couple of glasses of merlot, Jenny settled into the leather recliner and sighed happily as she sipped her third glass. "This is what I call quality, alone time," she said, giggling to herself as she watched some mindless romantic comedy from the fifties on the classics channel. The two glasses she had already consumed had relaxed her no end and also had the pleasant side effect of making her quite horny.

Jenny switched off the television and reclined further into the chair. She had changed after dinner, her hair was now pulled back in a ponytail and she was wearing one of Brad's white T-shirts. She loved the feel of the cotton on her bare breasts as she stretched like a cat, her nipples tingling and stiffening. She closed her eyes letting the sensation wash over her and squeezed her thighs together as she started to play one of her favourite fantasies through her head.

She teased herself like this a little longer, deliberately letting herself become more and more aroused. When she could bear it no longer she opened her legs a little and let her finger play lightly over her lacy panties, feeling the heat of her excitement through the inadequate material.

Her finger rubbed over the panties more insistently and they became wet with her lust. She played longer, teasing her clitoris through the lace then sliding a finger further down and pushing against her opening. Finally, she reached the point where the panties just had to come off and she raised her pelvis off the chair and began to slide them down her smooth thighs. She was just negotiating them past her knees when the doorbell startled her.

"Oh you are fucking kidding me!" she said aloud as she shot to her feet, heart thumping. She quickly and clumsily pulled her panties back up before straightening the T-shirt. It was barely long enough to cover her underwear so she quickly dragged on the pair of track pants that were draped over the sofa by the living room door and scurried out into the hallway. She paused briefly to look in the hallway mirror, patting her hair into a semblance of tidiness before moving on to the door.

She arrived at the front door and peered through the peep hole. To her horror she saw her sister's boyfriend of nine months, Mike Claven, standing there. Oh my God, she thought. What the hell does he want? She had never really taken to the dark haired and brooding southerner and was perplexed as to why he would be alone on her door step at this hour. She took a deep breath before pulling the door open.

"Well hello. What are you doing out and about at this hour Mike?"

Mike paused a moment, looking at her. He was well built and at six feet two, towered over her by four inches. She had always thought his mouth slightly cruel and it was no different when he smiled at her now.

"Just needed to show you something Jen, it couldn't wait," he said and bustled past her without waiting for an invitation. She noticed he was carrying a laptop bag.

"Oh okay, come on in then," she said ironically. He paused, letting her pass and she led him into the kitchen. Jenny felt a little tipsy and unsteady on her feet and her clitoris still tingled from her aborted play. She tried to make herself sound as normal as possible.

"Would you like a coffee or tea?" she asked. Mike shook his head and sat down at the dining table before opening the bag and slipping out his laptop computer.

"Won't be a second booting up," he said, his gaze lingering upon her for what seemed like a lifetime. This made her uncomfortable, but even though she felt he was acting strangely, she dismissed her feelings as alcohol fuelled paranoia.

She put the kettle on for herself and turned back to find him still looking at her with a smirk. "What's going on Mike?" she asked, for the first time becoming a little annoyed. She was taken aback when he patted the chair next to him, indicating she should sit.

"You'll see, just sit here so I can show you." Jenny contemplated his oddness for a moment before deciding to humour him. She sat next to him, trying to see the screen of the computer; it was still facing away from her.

"Now what you're going to see will shock you, so be prepared." Jenny looked quizzically at him; she had absolutely no idea what he was going to show her. He finally turned the laptop towards her so that she could see the screen.

A video began to play. It was her. On a webcam in a strange room, naked from the waist up, her mouth open in pleasure as her arm moved furiously at some task below the sight of the camera, it was very obvious what she was doing. Her heart began to thump in her chest. She felt as though her world was crumbling as she watched herself stand up from behind the desk and drop to her knees as a naked, tattooed man entered the scene. Tears started to stream down her face when the Jenny on screen started to slowly caress and kiss the penis of the newcomer. She couldn't speak for several seconds.

"Where the fuck did you get this?" she spat venomously.

"Doesn't really matter, does it?" he said, unpleasantly calm, "The fact is I have it, and you need to ask yourself what Brad would do if he saw it. His pristine wife sucking the cock of another man. It just doesn't bear thinking about, does it *Jennifer*?" Jenny flinched, as much at his use of her full name as what he had said. No-one called her that.

"That was a long time ago and none of your fucking business. Were you spying on me? Where did you get this?" she asked.

He laughed, "No, no don't be silly, nothing so perverted." He turned to the video watching her as she sucked the guy's big shaft expertly, before looking back to her, licking his lips suggestively. "My, my you're a naughty one Jennifer," he said and shook his head disapprovingly.

"I actually stumbled across it on a porn site, believe it or not. A site where guys upload videos of girls they've fucked, I just could not believe my luck when I saw you there! I mean I was fucking *amazed*!" He laughed again, shaking his head as though still in disbelief at his good fortune.

"What are you going to do with it? Show Brad?" snapped Jenny.

"Well not if you play your cards right. You would not believe how many times I've jerked off to this. Watching you take that load in your pretty mouth. Imagining what it would be like to blow my own load in you..." he placed his hand on her thigh.

She slapped his hand away and stood up suddenly, "Don't you dare touch me!"

"Really Jenny?" he stood up and leaned over her in a threatening manner. "You're not in a position to negotiate unfortunately. I would hate for Brad to open this on his work computer, could you imagine his face? I think we need to come to some kind of arrangement Jenny and soon or this video might just find its way to his email and to everyone else in his department too. You don't really want that do you Jenny?"

"Why would you do this? It was just after we were married, we were having problems. It was so long ago, Mike, please?" she pleaded.

He shrugged his shoulders in false sympathy before resuming his seat. "Well look at that would you?" She looked back to the screen just as 'video Jenny' pulled her mouth away from the enormous penis and took multiple squirts of semen into her mouth; it spilled down her chin as she smiled up at the unseen man, eagerly swallowing his offering.

"What do you want from me?" she said finally, defeated.

He stood up again and came over to her, "Your utter and complete submission. I've fantasised about you since the first time I met you, and I've always dreamed of having my very own sex slave." He reached up and tenderly caressed the side of her pretty face. "Who says dreams don't come true?" Jenny didn't respond as she thought furiously, trying to find a way out of this predicament.

Without warning Mike grabbed the neck of her T-shirt with two hands and tore it down the middle. Jenny gasped as her firm breasts jiggled in sudden freedom and she attempted to cover them, to little avail.

"My, my! Jennifer! Your nipples are hard; if I didn't know better I'd say you were horny." With that he pulled her hands roughly away from her breasts and down to her sides. "Leave them there," he ordered, as he admired her bare chest. He reached out a hand, cupping her left breast as he looked into her eyes challengingly. His cruel smile returned as he began to tease her nipple.

Jenny's body responded immediately to the stimulation, her nipples becoming even more erect. She cursed inwardly as her mind raced. She found no solution as she tried to ignore his hand. One email from Mike and her life was ruined. She could see the bulge in her sisters' boyfriend's jeans, and knew this was bad. Very bad.

"So what do you say Jen, do I send that email or do you consent to be my sex slave for as long as I want? I promise you will enjoy it." As if to emphasise this point, he leaned over and took Jenny's nipple in his mouth. The sensation of his warm mouth closing over her soft, sensitive skin sent a thrill of forbidden delight through her, she barely contained a cry of pleasure.

She had one last bullet to fire. "What about Olivia? You don't really want to do this to her, do you?" she pleaded breathlessly, now trying to ignore the insistent tongue flicking and teasing her nipple.

His mouth left her and he stood upright, drilling her with his gaze. "What Olivia doesn't know, won't hurt her," he said impatiently, "Now shall we do this? Or do I start sending emails."

"What do you want me to do?" She murmured, unable to look him in the eyes.

"For a start Jennifer, let's get the rest of your clothes off, I want to see the pussy that Brad's been pumping all these years." Jenny gasped. She couldn't believe her body was betraying her, aroused not only by the fact that she accepted his illicit proposal, but also by the way he was speaking to her.

They looked at each other a moment longer, Mike's face triumphant. He knew he had won. Defeated, and she hated to admit it, excited, she pulled the remnants of her t-shirt off and stood there. "Come on!" he urged hoarsely, "the track pants too." He grabbed the bulge in his jeans as he watched her. She pulled the track pants down and off, then straightened. Mike whistled through his teeth.

"*Great* body Jennifer... Whoa! What have we here? Your panties are wet!" He grabbed her chin and tilted her face up to his. "You *are* horny, you dirty little slut."

Still clamping her chin, he reached down and probed her panties with his index finger. It took all of her willpower not to moan as he watched her eyes intently. "Get your ass up on the table."

Jenny pulled herself onto the table top and gasped again as he moved quickly to push her legs apart, and not gently. Once again his fingers probed her wet panties pushing the lace into her warm opening. Jenny closed her eyes and let her head loll backwards to look at the ceiling. She was maintaining her composure, not moaning, hoping against hope that he would stop. It was not to be, he slid her panties to the side exposing the most precious and private part of her.

"Oh wow...yeah, that's gorgeous." He ran his bare finger from the top of her slit down over her clitoris and then further down, into her opening then up again. She squeezed her eyes shut, willing her body not to respond, trying to think of anything but what was happening.

He slapped her thigh lightly, "Ass up! Let's get those panties off." She lifted her backside and he slid the panties down her thighs and off, and then ordered her to open her mouth. She looked at him, "Please..." she begged in vain, but was cut short when he stuffed the panties into her mouth.

"Something for my slave to suck on while I eat her pussy," he whispered. He knelt in front of her and put his strong arms around her, pulling her along the table top towards him until her pussy was right over the edge.

She quickly looked upwards again trying to think of mundane things. She felt his tongue touch her clitoris and he began licking her up and down, around and around. This time she couldn't help groaning through the lace in her mouth. He sucked and licked her greedily and her body responded. Shocked at how easily she had succumbed, she determinedly tried to shut out the stimulation.

The longer it went on though, the less she could concentrate on trying to ignore it. He knew what he was doing down there, and she was helpless to switch off her body's response. Her mind began to reason out the situation. It was just one night wasn't it? To save her marriage it would be okay just this once, wouldn't it? What choice did she have?

She looked down at his face in her crotch and began to move her pelvis in time with his darting tongue. He pulled his mouth away and smiled coldly. "That's it whore, ride my tongue." He went back to it and she did just that, riding his face even more eagerly, stimulated by his nasty words. Finally, when she could bear it no longer she spat out the panties and groaned. But even through the haze of pleasure, Jenny was finding it hard to fathom she had succumbed to Mike's dark intentions so easily.

He suddenly ceased his ministrations and used the fingers of one hand to open her labia. He slid a finger into her opening and she moaned louder throwing her head back. The feel of his finger in her was too much and she pushed rhythmically against his hand. "Mmm," she breathed.

"You like that slut?"

"Mmm yes…" she looked down at him, lust heavy in her eyes.

She felt him slide another into her. By now she had lost any sense of guilt, all that mattered were the fingers inside her. The last of her resistance faded, and Jenny relaxed, immersing herself fully in the carnal action.

"Put more in, fuck me harder."

He laughed, shaking his head. She looked down and watched as he slid a third, finger into her...God she felt so full, but wanted more, she reached down and grabbed his wrist attempting to push him deeper and deeper into her.

When he spat onto her open sex, she was shocked at the act of debasement but also overcome with lust and quickly surrendered to her own primal cravings. "Oh yes! Oh my God, spit in me! Use me, I'm your slut!" She rode his fingers furiously, holding him inside her until she reached her climax, screaming in pleasure.

He withdrew his fingers from her and she leaned back, panting. "That's enough fun for you," he said mockingly, as he stood; "now it's my turn." He pulled off his jeans and she was surprised at the size of his manhood. He jerked her off the table, swung her around and then bent her face down over it.

"Spread your cheeks slut."

"Okay," she said submissively. She flinched when he suddenly cuffed the side of the head. "That's 'okay sir' to you." "Okay *sir*," she repeated, into the timber of the table, her flushed face hidden from him. She spread her cheeks as he had commanded and felt him spit into her again. His fingers found their way back inside her pussy, gliding in and out. She tensed as one slid into her ass, and then back down to her opening. He was using the moisture of her own body's excitement to lubricate her ass. Eventually the fingers seemed to take on a mind of their own, entering her vagina, then her ass, then out again. Both of her holes were now slippery with her fluids and his saliva.

"Slave, I'm going to use your pussy and your ass as I want, whenever I want, do you understand?" Once again Jenny moaned. "Yes sir...please, use them now." She had never felt so sinful, so wanton. He placed the head of his member against her slippery vaginal opening, waiting a moment before pushing it deep into her and with purpose. Jenny grunted in pleasure as his cock entered her and as he pumped her methodically she began to grind on his shaft, moaning again.

After a few minutes of thrusting into her, he said in a thick voice, "Uh, uh, Jennifer, I don't think so. As good as your cunt feels, it's not getting the first load." She sucked in a breath as she felt him withdraw abruptly from her and place the head of his penis against her ass, waiting only a second before unceremoniously pushing it into her.

She groaned in pain at first, no matter how many times she had asked, Brad had never been tempted to go in the 'backdoor' and she had only ever had a slim vibrator up there during her own private masturbation sessions. Jenny endeavoured to relax, embracing the rawness of the act, the sheer coarseness of it.

"Oh yeah, so tight." Mike said breathlessly. Luckily for Jenny her ass was well lubed and the alcohol had relaxed her, after the first few strokes the pain subsided. She began to enjoy the new sensation, the strange fullness and friction stimulating her in a way she hadn't expected.

"Oh my God, do me sir, do me in my ass." She reached under herself and began to play with her clitoris as he drove his shaft into her in steady thrusts. The feeling was amazing and she slowly began work towards another orgasm.

"Oh please fuck me sir. Harder! Cum in my virgin ass! I want to be your slave Mike!" she said hoarsely through gritted teeth.

He inhaled sharply at her words, and pumped her harder as they reached orgasm simultaneously. He groaned as he felt her writhe in climax and shot warm jets of his seed into her tight, virginal passage. After another few strokes he withdrew his still hard manhood and slipped it back into her womanly opening, and in the final throes of her own orgasm, she screamed in climactic pleasure as she accepted his shaft again. Satiated, Jenny collapsed faced down on the table with Mike resting on top of her, both panting.

After a few seconds, and without warning, he withdrew and ordered her off the table. He stepped back and gestured at his softening member. "You may suck me clean."

"Yes sir." She obediently dropped to her knees and took his now flaccid penis in her hands and slowly lapped at it, sucking and swallowing obediently. She felt it stiffening, and caressed it more eagerly.

"You have a good mouth whore, lick my balls clean too." She obeyed and licked at his balls diligently as he held his penis aside, allowing her access. A few seconds more of this and then he pushed her away and she fell to the side. "That's enough for now; you may get me a beer."

She nodded and whispered "yes sir."

"Good whore." He grabbed her by the hair before she could get up and leaned over as if to kiss her and instead, said "remember you are *my* slut now, and you are to do whatever I say without question. In return I will keep your secret safe and make sure you can live as normally as possible. Do you understand?" she felt utterly humiliated and still absolutely turned on. "Yes master."

"Good. Now, get me that beer." He released her and motioned towards the fridge.

Jenny got back to her feet a little unsteadily and walked to the refrigerator. She was in a daze. Now that the heat of her encounter with Mike was fading, disbelief at her own submission and her perverse enjoyment of being dominated sexually by Mike swirled through her mind. She thought briefly of Brad and Olivia, and then quickly shut them from her thoughts, wanting to savour the guilty pleasure for just a little longer. She pulled a beer from the fridge as Mike stood watching her, the cruel smile still etched on his face.

She walked back to him and he patted her on the cheek as she handed it to him, "Good girl." Jenny smiled in response. To her complete surprise he slapped her hard across the cheek.

"You will keep your eyes lowered slave. Speak to me only when spoken to. These are rules you must remember Jennifer, do you understand?"

Careful to keep her eyes lowered Jenny whispered "Yes master."

"Good, now let's go to your bedroom, I need to fuck you on the bed you share with your weak little man." He swigged deeply on the beer, before discarding the bottle. He quickly slid the computer back into its bag, and then picked up his jeans, carrying them both through the door to the hallway.

Jenny led the way to the stairs, still in shock at her own reaction to the humiliation she was enduring. There was something quite amazing about letting herself be dominated and debased, she had always been a strong independent woman, but the feelings she was experiencing were incredible, almost intoxicating.

He stopped her before she began up the stairs and leaned over, putting the laptop bag against the bottom step. "I forgot, I have something for you." She turned to see him pull a leather collar and leash from his jeans pocket. "Kneel before me."

Jenny did as he commanded and he fastened the collar around her neck as if she were a dog he was about to take for a walk. "Wow, you look amazing, naked and collared like that." She saw his penis start to grow again at the sight of her and felt her own sex respond. "Yes sir," she said meekly.

"Oh you and I are going to have so much fun. Come," he said, throwing the jeans down beside the laptop and stepped past her onto the stairs giving the leash a tug, "and stay on your knees."

She followed him up the stairs, and he pulled her along, guiding her into the main bedroom. "Oh yeah, here's where it all happens ladies and gentlemen," he announced, his cruel grin back.

"Mike please…" Jenny began to plead. Mike jerked her to her feet suddenly and put his face in hers. "What have I told you? Don't speak without being spoken to." With that he picked her up roughly and threw her on the bed, as if she weighed no more than a child.

He stood over her and began to stroke his newly engorged cock. "Open your pussy for me." Jenny moaned at his words and opened her legs. Reaching down she spread her labia wide. He clambered upon her and immediately began to thrust into her with a single minded determination.

She felt his breath, warm upon her face and he reached up pulling her hair so sharply that she had to arch her back to alleviate the pain, this had the effect of forcing him deeper into her. She gasped in agonised pleasure, which only seemed to excite him more.

"Mmm yeah take that you little whore, I bet your lame ass husband doesn't do it like this," his words were punctuated by his thrusting. Jenny, her desire again kindled, began to meet his thrusts motion for motion; his words and the feel of him inside her were too much to resist.

"Do it master, cum in me again, you're so much better than Brad….fuck me harder, oh my God I want to feel your cum dripping out of me." Jenny heard his breath quicken as he pushed into her with even more power and after a few more strokes he climaxed again.

Finally he fell beside her and they both lay there panting. After a few minutes he looked over to her. "Don't worry about cleaning me again, I'm going to put my cock in your sister tonight, she won't have any idea that it'll have your pussy all over it."

A pang of guilt ran through Jenny. Then disgust. Disgust at herself and at Mike, and also at what they had done. She didn't respond, she didn't want to encourage this type of talk, but also didn't want to bring his wrath down upon her by protesting. Finally he got out of the bed.

"Retrieve my jeans, I have to get moving."

Jenny ran down the stairs and returned with them. After pulling them on, he approached her and put his hands around her neck. She tensed and was relieved when all he did was remove the collar.

"All right. You're mine forever, not only do I have the video, I've given you the fuck of your life, there really is no going back now." He laughed as he patted her cheek again and headed out of the room.

She came out of the bedroom and stood on the landing watching as he went down the stairs. He turned around and looked up at her. "I'll be in touch. Keep your mouth shut if you know what's good for you." She watched him pick up the laptop and go to the front door. He didn't look back as he went through, slamming the door behind him.

After he had gone, Jenny, still dazed, walked back into her bedroom and sat on the bed. There was a ball of dread in her stomach at the predicament she was in, but behind that there was also excitement. Anticipation of what Mike had in store for her. "What the fuck is wrong with me" she asked herself aloud. He had used and treated her like the worst slut, a sex toy and she had loved it. No-one had ever spoken to her like that, and she was flabbergasted that she could in any way find it a turn on. But she did. While sex with Brad had never been boring, with him she had never experienced the pure lust and absolute release that she had tonight. Oh my God, I am a slut, she thought.

Jenny showered and went back downstairs, still in a daze, and tried to rationalise what had happened as she poured herself a bourbon. She had been drunk, and it had literally been over a month since she and Brad had had sex. She was sexually frustrated, not to mention dissatisfied with her relationship and life in general. That had to be it, right? So she had lost control...it wasn't like she had seduced Mike. He had blackmailed her, what choice did she have?

She began to feel better as the alcohol warmed her. Would he really try this again? Surely not, it was too risky. She finished her drink and went to bed. She lay for over an hour, tossing and turning. Not thinking about Brad. Not feeling guilty. Instead she fantasised about what might happen if and when Mike did call upon her again. Jenny didn't know it then, but not even her darkest sexual fantasies would scratch the surface of what was to come.

<u>Notes</u>

Sharing Emma

Jeremy Daniels arrived at Whittaker's. He had been waiting tables at the five star restaurant for ten months now and had never been late. Today he was running just two minutes late but was worried, the head waiter Johnson was scrupulous about such things. The darkly handsome twenty-four year old bustled through the rear entrance, and headed immediately for the staff change room.

To his dismay, the perpetually unhappy looking Johnson was the first person he saw as he entered. It was a miserable rainy night out in London and his dark hair was plastered to his head. He skidded to a halt in front of his immaculately attired superior and mumbled "Sorry I'm late sir." To his relief Johnson merely nodded and ushered him away. Once in the safety of the change room he removed his civilian clothes quickly and efficiently and dressed in his tails.

After dressing and making his hair presentable, he left the change room and reported to Johnson. The restaurant in which they worked was a contradiction, on one hand it was one of the most popular in the city and yet, by all accounts was also one of the least crowded and most intimate. Prospective customers had to book nearly a year in advance to secure a table and patronage was almost exclusively from the nouveau rich and upper class along with a spattering of celebrities.

Whittaker's waiters never had to wait more than two tables at a time so that patrons received the personal service they were paying so handsomely for. While he himself was from a working middle class family, Jeremy's confidence, good looks and penchant for dealing with even the worst snobs in a personal non subservient way soon had him waiting the restaurant's two best tables. They were located in an area known as 'the nook'.

'The nook' was a small room sized alcove with two windows overlooking the city; these tables were the most sought after in the restaurant. It was a part of, yet distinct and slightly distant from the main dining area and seemed to have an atmosphere of its own.

Upon reporting to Johnson he was told that both tables in 'The nook' had been reserved but only one couple would be dining. Jeremy had looked quizzically at Johnson, who in an annoyed tone advised him that the customer had paid a premium for the privilege and no further questions were to be asked.

Just after 8pm Jeremy saw Johnson escorting a couple to 'the nook'. Jeremy watched them discreetly as they got settled. The man was a distinguished looking gent in his late sixties, and the girl, who looked about twenty-one and probably young enough to be his granddaughter, was a stunning blonde, her hair hanging stylishly to her shoulders. She was wearing a red coat over a black dress and a thick a gold choker around her neck.

Jeremy made some assumptions about the couple as they weaved their way towards the table, firstly they were definitely not a grandfather or father daughter team, the gentleman's hand was placed intimately low on the girls back as he guided her to the table. Secondly the girl seemed extremely meek towards the man, clearly a young girl overwhelmed by the man and the setting.

When this woman's coat came off, Jeremy was pleasantly surprised, the girl had an amazing figure and the clingy black dress showed off her curves nicely. The dress was shoulder less and her perfect cream toned skin contrasted the black of the dress beautifully. She didn't appear to have on any jewellery beside the choker as far as he could tell. When the two sat down the man said something quietly to her and she smiled before lowering her eyes. She seemed very obsequious.

After Johnson had handed them the menus and retreated Jeremy started over to them. The young waiter stopped in shock when the young lady leaned over the table parting her lips as the man reached forward and inserted his index finger into her waiting mouth. What followed was the most amazing thing he had ever seen in the restaurant. The girl drew the man's finger into her mouth and proceeded to suck it as though she were sucking a cock. Her head bobbed back and forth, a look of absolute pleasure on her face. Jeremy was transfixed, watching her perfect mouth and the now glistening finger move in and out of it. He felt his manhood start to stir at the sight.

He was snapped out of his reverie when he realised that the man was looking directly at him, a slight smile on his face, as the pretty young thing continued to suck his finger. Jeremy looked away like a guilty schoolboy and brushed at non-existent lint on his suit before resuming his walk to the table. Thankfully by the time he arrived the man had removed his finger from his date's mouth.

"Good evening sir, madam, I am Jeremy and I will be your waiter for this evening." The young lady's eyes remained lowered to the table; Jeremy's gaze was drawn to the swell of her bosom which was nicely showcased by the low cut dress. The man acknowledged him. "Hello Jeremy, you're a strapping looking lad. Look I'll cut to the chase, I'm not interested in the wine list, bring me a double scotch on the rocks, and nothing for the slut."

Jeremy did a double take and decided that he had misheard. The girl, even more beautiful up close, hadn't reacted and still sat quietly staring down at the table. Very odd, he thought. He took their meal orders and with some relief retreated to the kitchen.

Jeremy returned to the table a few minutes later and placed the drink in front of the old man. "Your entrée will be served shortly sir," he advised. He was about to return to the kitchen when the man said "Jeremy, this is Emma. Lovely creature isn't she?"

Jeremy froze, unsure if this was a trap or not. In a split second he decided that he had to respond either way, he looked at the girl, still sitting with eyes down, and said honestly, "Yes sir she is."

"Glad you think so. Look up at Jeremy and say hello slut," he ordered the girl. Jeremy's mouth formed a perfect O of surprise as he processed the insult. The girl looked up at him bashfully. Her stunning green eyes met his, "Hello Jeremy," before they returned to the table.

Jeremy was amazed at her non reaction and looked at the man. He was smiling mischievously, almost challengingly at Jeremy, who fought with himself about saying something in the beauty's defence. "Show him your cunt, whore."

Jeremy sputtered, "Now sir, I don't think that's appr…" the words dried up in his mouth as the girl pulled out her chair daintily, swung it around to face Jeremy, hiked up her dress a little and then spread her wonderful legs.

Once again she raised her beautiful green eyes to Jeremy and smiled. Jeremy's manhood didn't just move this time, he sprouted an almost instant hard on as he eyed the girls perfect pussy, it was smooth and devoid of hair. Jeremy looked over his shoulders, and moved surreptitiously to ensure that no one else would spy what was happening.

"What do you think my boy?" the older man asked. "Hot little thing isn't she." Jeremy licked his lips, "Yes sir…amazing." He shuffled were he stood attempting to get his raging erection into a comfortable and less noticeable position.

The old man snapped his fingers and the girl pulled her dress back down and returned her chair back to its original position. Her gaze returned to the table. Jeremy stood where he was for a moment, his mind blank.

"Go on with you,' said the man, "see to our entrees now that you've had yours." He laughed out loud at his own humour. Jeremy, still in a state of shock left the table and went back to the kitchen.

Jeremy's mind started to race with possibilities. It was obvious that something was at play. He didn't know much about sex slaves but it appeared the girl called Emma was playing that sort of part. It was going to be an interesting night. He wondered if the old man would make her do anything else. Perhaps the rich couple had just decided to have some fun with the waiter to ease their affluent boredom.

By the time he returned to the table with the entrees his hard on had subsided, and he felt as though he had some sort of control back. He was going to play it by ear, but if it turned out they were not playing games with him, he was going to take full advantage of the situation. Opportunities like this only came along once in a lifetime. Besides, if the girl wanted to be used by an old pervert, why should he get all uptight about it?

His basest hopes were confirmed when he was just about to leave after placing the couple's entrées in front of them. "Jeremy, just one moment if you would?"

"Certainly sir.'

"I only allow Emma certain types of fluid. Be a good lad and spit in my dogs mouth for me would you?" Once again Jeremy was shocked silent and stood frozen to the floor. The girl looked up at him and opened her mouth. Jeremy didn't think he had ever seen anything so sexy, her red lipstick was still smudged from the performance on the old man's finger and her perfect teeth glistened.

"Come along, don't be shy, you won't be caught out. Just lean over her and do it." Jeremy's hard-on had returned and the fact that this absolute beauty had her mouth open almost begging for him to debase her, was driving him wild.

"Really?" he asked her. She smiled and nodded before opening her mouth wide again. His heart thumped with a shot of adrenalin. He sloshed his tongue around producing saliva and leaned over her as requested. A white gob of spit fell into her mouth and slid down her tongue, she immediately closed her mouth smiling at him and swallowing it as if she was savouring the world's finest wine.

"Isn't she something, Jeremy?" Sure now that this was not some kind of prank, Jeremy responded, "She is quite something sir."

"Give her some more will you? She must be thirsty." Once again the girl opened her mouth and looking around nervously, Jeremy made sure he wasn't being watched and spat again into the girl's mouth. "Don't swallow it," the man commanded, Jeremy could see the saliva sitting on her tongue. "Go ahead and finger her mouth if you like."

Jeremy's erection was raging against his trousers as he tentatively put his finger into the girl's mouth. "Come on lad don't be shy, put two in." He did as the old man suggested and the girl's lips closed gently around his two fingers and he began to thrust them slowly in and out. The waiter was now as aroused as he had ever been in his whole life, standing in a five start restaurant, fingering the mouth of an absolutely gorgeous woman. He slid another finger into her mouth, fingering her harder, feeling her teeth rough against his knuckles. He lost himself in the moment and thrust them deeper and was gratified to hear her gag a little.

The sight of his three fingers buried in her mouth was amazing and the old boy was clearly enjoying the show. He placed a hand on Jeremy's wrist and pushed hard on the next thrust, making the girl gag again and her eyes water.

"All right that's enough for now lad. Just wipe your fingers in her hair, we can't have that unsightly mess on your hands now can we?" Jeremy reluctantly took his fingers out of her mouth and wiped them on her hair as though it were a dish rag.

"All right you may eat now whore. Jeremy, thank you, you may leave us until you serve the main meals."

"Yes sir," Jeremy said and glanced one more time at the girl, she was looking down at the table again, strands of her formerly immaculate hair now marred with dampness. She picked up her fork and began to eat the small salad the old man had ordered for her.

Jeremy visited the staff men's room to wash his hands and splash cold water on his face. He was very tense, trying to balance his duties and professional demeanour against the pure debauchery he was experiencing courtesy of the beautiful girl and her benefactor. He towelled off and went to help in the kitchen as he waited until he could go and clear the entrée plates.

He left the kitchen door and looked surreptitiously to 'The nook', only to find the man gesturing for him to come over. He felt dread mixed with butterflies of excitement in his middle. "Sorry to be such a nuisance Jeremy, but Emma so enjoyed you spitting in her pretty mouth and fingering it for her, that she got very aroused, isn't that right, my dear?"

"Yes master," she whispered.

"Jeremy, hold off on clearing the plates away would you? You've seen my slut's pussy and obviously enjoyed it, would you like to give it a licking? Right now, under the table, a one-time opportunity."

"Yes sir, it would be my pleasure, but perhaps somewhere more private?" Jeremy said after some hesitation.

"No, no, my boy. Perhaps at a later stage, but this one is in training, and one of the things she must get used to, is being used by strangers in public places. Now what do you say? Just come around here on the window side of the table, duck down and you'll be out of sight. I can give warning if anyone comes this way. That sweet cunt is yours right now if you want it."

Once again Jeremy looked at the young woman, her eyes watched him but she offered no guidance. "Don't bother asking the dog silly, she will do whatever I tell her to do, it's all down to you old son."

"Okay, yes I want her pussy." Once again he had a raging hard-on and moved around the table until he was next to the girl. Jeremy heard the man telling Emma to spread her legs. She moved her chair again so it was facing him and had her back to the rest of the dining room. She obeyed her master parting her creamy inner thighs and as she did so, her dress rode high up her thighs. He was once again faced with the prettiest little pussy he'd ever seen. He licked his lips automatically and kneeled in front of her open legs.

She was definitely aroused; he could see her pink slit glistening moistly and she smelled wonderfully musky. He could bear it no longer and reached out and tentatively ran his finger over Emma's slit. Then again, with slightly more pressure so that the tip of his finger slipped between her labia. He circled her opening, collecting more and more moisture and couldn't resist doing the same thing to her clit.

He half crawled under the table and she moved her chair slightly back to face her master, above him, he heard her quiet voice and thought it was almost cruel for the man to make her talk calmly about her day while she was being teased. Now that her hole was lubricated he slid a finger into her and was pleasantly surprised at how tight she was. She thrust forward almost involuntarily and started to gently ride his finger. Unable to wait any longer he removed his finger and put his hands on her hips and slid her forward on the seat towards his face. He pushed her thighs even further apart before greedily plunging his mouth into her pussy.

He licked her slit from top to bottom, paying particular attention to her clitoris and as her thrusting became more urgent, his tongue responded. He swallowed her juice as he licked and teased her and was almost unbearably aroused. For a moment he thought it possible he might just blow his load into his trousers. Finally he felt the girl orgasm, her pussy tensed as he slid his finger back into her for the climax. After she had relaxed, he withdrew his finger, and tenderly kissed her pussy before emerging from under the white tablecloth.

He stood there slightly sheepish. The old man smiled at him before looking at Emma. "What do you say to the young man, slut?"

"Thank you for pleasuring me sir."

Jeremy mumbled "You're welcome," and started to clear the entrée plates. He saw several patrons glancing in his direction and was not sure whether to be paranoid, or if it was just natural curiosity about the old man and his young 'date'. Of course they may have been wondering what he had been doing down there for so long and he prayed it wasn't that obvious what he had been up to.

The next ten minutes passed uneventfully, no one complained and he wasn't fired or escorted from the premises. Jeremy was called when the main meal was ready and skilfully picked up the plates and headed back to the table. He was disappointed to find that Emma had disappeared.

The old man winked at him and nodded down at the table suggestively, before rolling his eyes in obvious pleasure. Jeremy was full of admiration for the old boy's balls of steel, he was really something. Jeremy waited patiently and not two minutes later the old boy straightened in his seat and let out a deep sigh. A few seconds later the girl crawled out from under the table and resumed her seat, her eyes dropping to the table.

"Sorry old boy, I was just allowing Emma here some more fluids. Show young Jeremy your treat," he said looking at the girl. The girl looked up to the ceiling and opened her mouth, it was filled with the old man's cum. "She's not allowed to swallow it until I permit her. How good does that pretty little mouth look filled with that?"

"Amazing sir."

"Do you think she looks thirsty? I think she does. Swallow a little of it slut, but leave some on your tongue, poke it right out for all to see." The girl obeyed and partially swallowed the mouthful, then poked her tongue out, the dregs of the old man's semen glistening on the pink flesh.

"There's a good dog. Okay you may swallow the rest and begin eating. That will be all for now Jeremy, bring me another scotch will you?"

Jeremy made his way back to the kitchen, again amazed at what he had witnessed. This girl was totally subservient to the old man. She had no shame. His balls ached and he thought briefly of going into the staff men's room to relieve himself, but the possibility that the old man might share more of his bitch prevented him, he wanted to be up and ready for it if the time came.

Eight minutes later Jeremy returned to the table with the two main meals and a scotch for the old man. Jeremy paused for a moment, but the couple started eating and he sensed that nothing was going to happen. He headed back to the kitchen.

When one of the waitresses he normally flirted with commented that he seemed preoccupied, he brushed it off. His mind was definitely preoccupied with only one woman tonight.

The rest of the evening passed without any further excitement, and Jeremy was resigned to the fact that he had had some fun with the very interesting couple, but that the little display he had enjoyed was probably the extent of it.

The main meal had been finished, desserts served and now the old man was on his second round of coffee. They stretched it on and on, so much so that Jeremy began to wonder what they could be doing to keep themselves amused for so long. Every time he looked over or visited the table the couple did not seem to be talking at all, although the old man did take several long phone calls.

The other diners had gradually disappeared until there was now only one other table still occupied. They were an attractive young couple who were dressed to kill and had been petting, making eyes at each other and downing glasses of champagne like there was no tomorrow .

The wait and kitchen staff had been gradually completing their shifts for the evening and Jeremy began to resent the fact that his personal time was now being encroached upon.

Finally the old man waved at him indicating he should bring the cheque. Mumbling "About time," under his breath Jeremy went to the cashier to have it prepared. The other young couple appeared oblivious to the time and it appeared the waiter for their table wouldn't be going anywhere soon.

Jeremy walked with purpose to the old man's table and handed him the bill. "Thank you old boy, the meal and the service were excellent," he handed Jeremy ten crisp one hundred pound notes, "keep the change for yourself." Jeremy was stunned, this was the biggest tip by far that he had ever received.

"Thank you sir," he said, genuinely appreciative.

"You're welcome. Now have most of the staff cleared out for the evening?" The old man asked him.

"Yes sir, just a few of us left," looking around, he could see an impatient Johnson on the edges of the dining room glaring at the smitten couple.

"Good. Come to me bitch," he ordered Emma loudly. Jeremy stepped aside and allowed the girl to sidle up to the old man, who had now risen from his seat. Jeremy was totally unprepared for what followed. In a swift move the old man grabbed the girls dress above the swell of her bosom, and using both hands ripped it asunder. The sound of tearing fabric rent the room and everyone turned towards the standing couple.

There were gasps of surprise from the female diner and her partner, who had finally torn their eyes from each other to look at the now naked Emma. Jeremy was helpless not to look, the girls fantastic breasts still jiggled slightly after the dress containing them had been violently ripped away.

As she stood naked, the object of attention for everyone in the room, the old man reached into his pocket and pulled out a leash. Jeremy saw Johnson over the shoulder of the old man, making a bee line for them and prepared for impact.

"What is going on here sir?" demanded the head waiter officiously as he shuddered to a stop. Johnson became almost apoplectic when the old man told him to hush as he clasped the lead to the girl's choker, which Jeremy now realised was actually a collar, not an item of jewellery.

The old man turned to Jeremy and handed him the leash, "Mind my dog for me will you?"

Johnson sucked a deep breath ready to unleash a tirade when the old man turned to him and pulled out his wallet. "Here is five thousand pounds for the use of this establishment for an hour or so," without waiting for an answer he started thumbing one hundred pound notes into Johnson's hand, which had miraculously gone from a pointing finger into an open palm, "see that it pays for that handsome young couples meal, and share it with the staff that haven't gone home, there's a good lad." Johnson mumbled of course sir, under his breath.

"Good, now that we've got that business sorted out, have all of your staff but Jeremy here finish up for the night, he can lock up for you. This young couple may stay if they like." An odd silence had descended over the remaining staff and guests. Both the man and the woman were staring avidly at the naked beauty and watching what was taking place between the old man and the staff. The young man looked to his date who gave a small shrug indicating her approval.

Johnson gave Jeremy a look that promised trouble in the near future, before he handed him the keys to the restaurant. "Make sure you do all of the end of evening tasks, and be here early tomorrow evening to hand me the keys before opening." Jeremy nodded, not quite knowing how to feel as he stood facing his superior while holding the leash of an extremely sexy and very naked woman. To his relief, Johnson didn't tarry, he turned on his heel and waved to the young couple's waiter and they both headed to the kitchen.

The whole time these negotiations were taking place, Emma stood obediently looking at the floor, her cheeks tinged with a flush of embarrassment.

"All right then," said the old man, "on your knees where you belong, slut." The young woman at the other table gasped again at his words but Emma did not flinch, she dropped to her hands and knees immediately.

"Very good," he said as he retrieved the leash from Jeremy. He led the girl on her hands and knees over to the tipsy couple. "Would you like to pet it?" He asked them both. Once again the male looked to his partner for approval but was surprised when in answer; she reached out herself to caress the collared girl's breast. Needing no further encouragement the man reached under Emma to grab her other breast. The old man twitched the leash and Emma obediently lifted herself back onto her haunches so that the couple could access her chest more easily.

"Nice aren't they?" the old man asked. They continued to caress the girl, as she sat on her haunches with eyes to the floor. "Would you like to use her mouth young man?"

The man's date looked at him and nodded. "Damn straight I would," he said enthusiastically, rising to his feet hurriedly. Watching intently, Jeremy leaned back against the table opposite them, his own rock hard cock aching as the male diner pulled his erect member out of his pants and shuffled toward the naked girl. His date also moved in and watched Emma raise her chin and open her mouth for her date's cock.

Jeremy watched as the beautiful Emma took the offered penis in her mouth and began to expertly suck it. The woman continued to rub and tease the slave's breasts as her man began thrusting into Emma's mouth. When the female diner began caressing herself under her dress Jeremy decided it was time to get his own cock out. He lightly stroked it as the woman pinched Emma's nipple hard, drawing a groan of pain from her. In response the male diner moaned in pleasure at the tightening of the slave's mouth.

This went on for a while before the man's breathing quickened and his more urgent thrusting indicated he was close to climax. He was about to blow his load when the girlfriend interrupted, pulling him out of Emma's mouth and swallowing his cock with her own pretty lips. This was too much for her partner and he blew his load into her mouth, his hips thrusting as he shuddered to orgasm.

His date pushed him away and grabbed Emma's face and began kissing her deeply and vigorously, Jeremy could see cum and saliva coating their lips and had to slow his stroking in order not to go beyond the point of no return.

Jeremy glanced at the old man, who had retired to a chair to watch the action, Jeremy was impressed that he appeared to have a raging boner, this show was definitely better than Viagra.

The male diner had also retired to a chair looking spent; his date however was still tonguing the slave's mouth oblivious to anyone else in the room.

The old man seemed to grow impatient. "Would you like my dog to eat you out young lady?"

The girl broke away from her embrace with Emma and nodded with lust heavy in her eyes. She retreated to the chair beside her husband and slipped off her panties before sitting down and spreading her svelte legs.

The old man got up and led Emma over to the waiting woman before grabbing her hair roughly and pushing her face into the woman's crotch. The slave began licking and sucking at the woman's pussy and Jeremy was not surprised to see the old man fiddling with his trousers. He was however surprised a few seconds later when in one quick motion the old man pulled out, not his cock, but his belt and whipped Emma's ass with it. Emma's scream was muffled by the woman's pussy and again at the second stroke. The female diner moaned in ecstasy at this new development and panted, "Yeah whip that bitches ass."

"That's right pig; suck this stranger's cunt while I whip your ass for no good reason. You're mine to do with as I please, and don't forget it," rasped the old man harshly.

He kept whipping Emma's ass with slow strokes and the woman quickly reached orgasm, clearly stimulated by the pain being inflicted on the young girl. She ripped at Emma's hair, pulling her pretty face deeper into her pussy as she writhed to climax.

The old man ceased whipping after the woman had pushed Emma away and pulled her back to her feet by the leash. He led her around the two exhausted diners to the end of their table and swept the plates from it. Everyone jumped as the fine china plates smashed on the polished timber floor.

"All right young Jeremy, your turn now, I've saved the best for you. Now, while her cunt has been used before, it's never had a cock in it. No need to be gentle though, that gorgeous pussy is one of the main reasons I purchased her, so feel free to enjoy."

The old man pushed his slave backwards onto the table ensuring her ass was right on the edge before stepping aside. He waved Jeremy towards her, as she laid back and spread her legs. Still demure; her eyes seemed to be diverted whenever Jeremy looked at her. He drank in the sight of her perfect body and open sex and impossibly, his cock seemed to grow even harder.

Jeremy slid a finger into her inviting pussy and was surprised at how wet she was, she responded immediately and began to gently fuck his finger. He slid another one in and she moved harder against them. The sudden crack of the belt across those perfect breasts shocked Jeremy and the girl screamed in surprise. The girl looked up at her master, "More please sir."

The old man brought the belt down again and again and the girl moaned in pleasure and pain, now thrusting her pelvis against Jeremy's fingers. He could tolerate it no longer, and mounted her, moaning in absolute pleasure as he entered the tightest pussy he had ever been in.

He began fucking her slowly at first, relishing the sight of her face as it contorted in ecstasy. He looked up briefly and saw that the male diner was now fucking his date doggy style as they greedily watched the show.

Jeremy focussed his attention back on Emma; the flawless skin of her breasts was pink from the punishment of the belt. He tried to hold out, but the stimulation was too great, this perfect fuck toy, the situation and the feel of her tight cunt were too much. He tried to withdraw as he started to climax but Emma sensing this, clamped her thighs around him and forced him deeper into her. They both groaned in ecstasy as he continued thrusting until he had spent every last drop of himself in her.

He collapsed on top of her as he heard the other couple reach their own happy ending. He lay there for a few minutes, breathing into her sweaty neck, aware of the old man replacing his belt and straightening himself up. "That's enough young Jeremy, well done. Don't worry about having cum in her by the way, she uses contraceptives."

Jeremy propped himself up and gently kissed the slightly open lips of the girl under him. She responded in kind, before breaking off the kiss. Jeremy stood up and began to put his uniform back in order. The two diners now appeared quite self-conscious and said hurried goodbyes and left after Jeremy pointed to the kitchen and advised them how to find the rear exit.

"Up you get dog, make yourself decent," said the old man to his slave. Emma obeyed instantly and was presentable in a couple of minutes, she had put on the red coat which barely covered her ass and picked up the remnants of her ruined dress and clutch. The old man grabbed the leash and began to lead her out the same way the other couple had exited.

"Well that was lovely old boy," he said conversationally to Jeremy, "compliments to the chef. You as well my boy," at the door he turned to Jeremy and handed him a business card, "if you're ever interested for yourself, get in touch. Take care of yourself my boy."

Jeremy watched them go and tried to catch Emma's eye as she followed the old man with her head bowed. He was disappointed when she didn't even acknowledge him. He came to the realisation that she was entirely in the old man's thrall and that it didn't matter who had used her that night, there was no attachment apart from the one to her master.

Jeremy looked down at the card, it was high quality and embossed in gold. "Colonel Jacob Meredith, Purveyor of the finest domestic and exotic helpers". It included a number and email address at the bottom. Jeremy smiled, and thought of the world of possibilities this card just might open for him…

<u>Notes</u>

Thanks again for purchasing *How to Write Erotic Short Stories that Sell*, the following page contains my catalogue and further examples of my short stories.

Christina.

Christina Palmer Catalogue

The Bad cop
The Bad Cop Pays a Visit
The Bad Cop Takes a Bride

Duty Bound – The Enslavement of Jenny

Part 1 Taking Jenny

Part 2 Training Jenny

Part 3 Breaking Jenny

Part 4 Sharing Jenny

Part 5 Punishing Jenny

Part 6 Jenny Unbound

Naughty Housewives

Touch Me There Doctor!

While the Cat's Away

Use my Wife…Please

One off stories

The Bad Doctor

Sharing Emma

Violating Prisoner X

29556956R00044

Made in the USA
Lexington, KY
29 January 2014